Red Grooms

and the Heroism of Modern Life

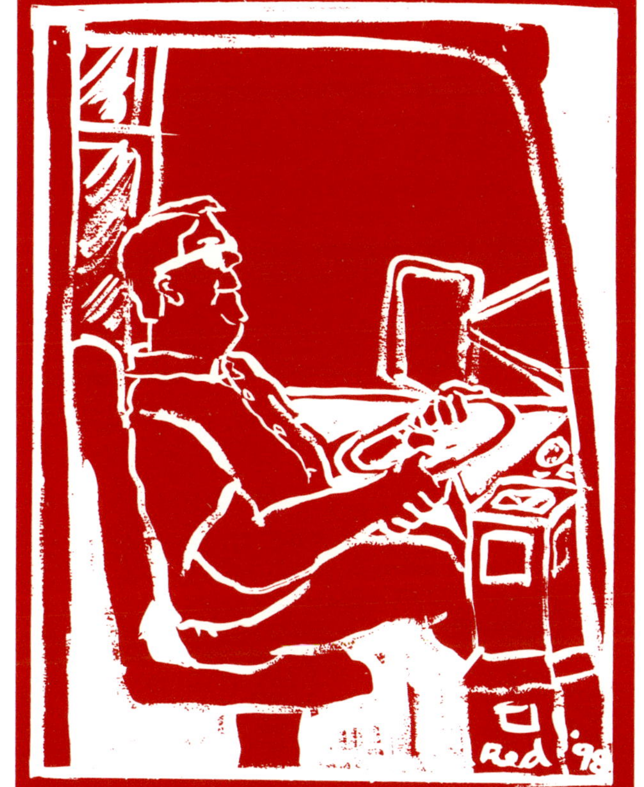

. . . The crowd is his domain, just as the air is the bird's, and water that of the fish. His passion and his profession is to merge with the crowd. For the perfect idler, for the passionate observer it becomes an immense source of enjoyment to establish his dwelling in the throng, in the ebb and flow, the bustle, the fleeting and the infinite. To be away from home and yet to feel at home anywhere; to see the world, to be at the very centre of the world, and yet to be unseen of the world, such are some of the minor pleasures of those independent, intense and impartial spirits, who do not lend themselves easily to linguistic definitions.

— Charles Baudelaire,
"The Painter of Modern Life," (1859)[1]

PALMER MUSEUM OF ART

September 12 — December 23, 1998

"The Man of the Crowd"

Red Grooms **is an artist who,**

like Baudelaire's painter of modern life, has never lent himself easily to "linguistic definitions." Throughout his career he has been labeled a maverick, a court jester, and a hard-to-pigeonhole one-man movement. As early as 1973 he was designated "the favorite 'out' artist of the 'in' New York scene" by an influential *New York Times* critic.[3] Since the 1960s his work has appeared regularly at major New York City galleries and at museums throughout the world. His zany take on life—"ruckus" is the term he and scholars use to characterize it—is evident in every piece he creates, from two-dimensional prints and drawings to his signature walk-through environments. "I have a streak of show business in me," the artist acknowledges.[4] And what a show it is.

It may seem odd to call upon Baudelaire, that most notorious and at times macabre of nineteenth-century French essayists, to help us decipher the marvelous spectacle of Grooms' art. But there Baudelaire is, lurking somewhere in the seemingly fathomless recesses of the artist's imagination and given form in a suite of prints titled *Nineteenth-Century Artists* published by the artist in 1976. Grooms' depiction of the poet is macabre indeed: the head of the decapitated writer appears on a platter swung about by a Salome-like femme fatale. The sparsely bejeweled nude extends her tongue in a strange, not-altogether-sexual pose, visually evoking, it would seem, one of the poet's famous "flowers of evil." Conversely, lewd is the only way to describe the tongue wagging occurring in Grooms' rendering of Constantin Guys from the same portfolio. Guys' lurid gaze is directed toward the naked model before him, a pose in keeping with the general lascivious tenor of the entire suite but seemingly at odds with Baudelaire's well-known characterization of the artist in "The Painter of Modern Life."

For Baudelaire, Guys was *the* quintessential artist of modern life. Little discussed outside of scholarly circles today, Guys was a French artist-journalist who covered newsworthy events, including the Crimean War, for the *Illustrated London News*. Largely self-taught, Guys worked outside the official salon system and was known in his day for his rapidly sketched drawings and watercolors of elegant Parisians promenading along the boulevards of Second Empire Paris. As early as 1845, Baudelaire had called for just such an artist, one who could capture the ephemeral beauty of fashionable modern city life.

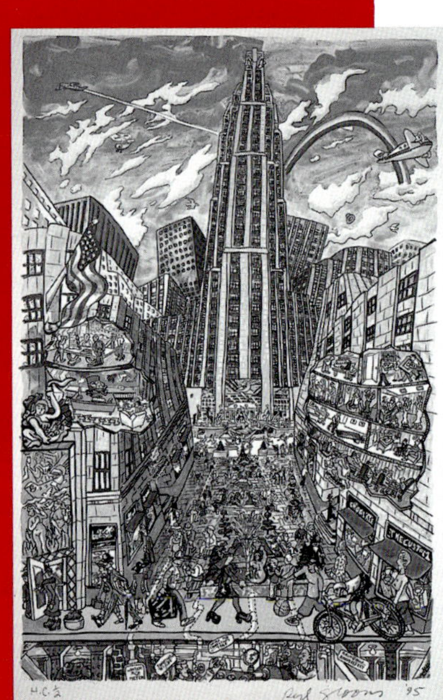

Rockefeller Center, 1995
(cat. 32)

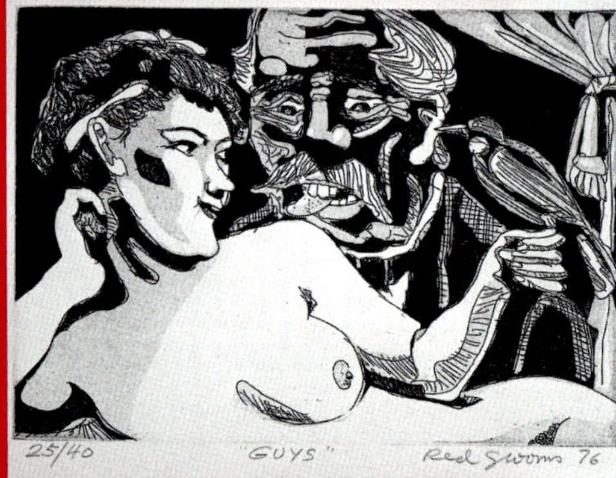

Nineteenth-Century Artists: Guys, 1976, etching and aquatint, 14 7/8 x 11 inches; Portfolio of 10, edition of 40. Published by Brooke Alexander Gallery and Marlborough Graphics; printed by Jennifer Melby.

> **T**here is no lack of subjects, nor of colours, to make epics. The painter, the true painter for whom we are looking, will be he who can snatch its epic quality from the life of today and can make us see and understand, with brush or pencil, how great and poetic we are in our cravats and our patent-leather boots.[5]

At this early moment

in his career as art critic, Baudelaire had yet to find the artist who would adequately convey what he called "the heroism of modern life." One year later in his review of the annual salon, in a concluding section pointedly titled "On the Heroism of Modern Life," the young poet announced once again his call for an artist capable of seizing the epic or heroic qualities of modern life. "Our age is no less rich than ancient times in sublime themes," the poet argues. "It may be asserted that since every age and every people have had their own form of beauty, we inevitably have ours. That is the order of things."[6]

By 1859, when Baudelaire penned his thoughts in "The Painter of Modern Life," the delightfully of-the-moment drawings of Guys had come to his attention. Referred to throughout the essay as "M.G." (for "Monsieur Guys") at the insistence of the reticent artist, Guys satisfied Baudelaire's desire for an "artist-portrayer of manners" capable of depicting the fleeting moment in a style that seemingly was itself transient or in flux. "There is in the trivial things of life, in the daily changing of external things, a speed of movement that imposes upon the artist an equal speed of execution."[7] Baudelaire's explication of modernity as "the transient, the fleeting, the contingent" works hand-in-hand with his historical theory of beauty, also developed in the essay, which, simply stated, holds that each age has its own "particular" form of beauty. The painter able to extract this circumstantial beauty from the life around him thus captures the "heroism" of modern life, conveying to future generations the "epic" quality of a particular time and place.

For Baudelaire, Guys was importantly a "man of crowds"; that is, a man passionately engaged in the world yet sufficiently "dandified" to maintain the critical distance required of the astute observer. The true contemporary artist's "passion and profession is to merge with the crowd," the poet contends, "dwelling in the throng, in the ebb and flow, the bustle, the fleeting and the infinite."

At home at the very center of the world, Guys was for Baudelaire the perfect artist-*flâneur*, the inveterate stroller constantly in motion and perpetually enthralled by the rich spectacle of modern life.

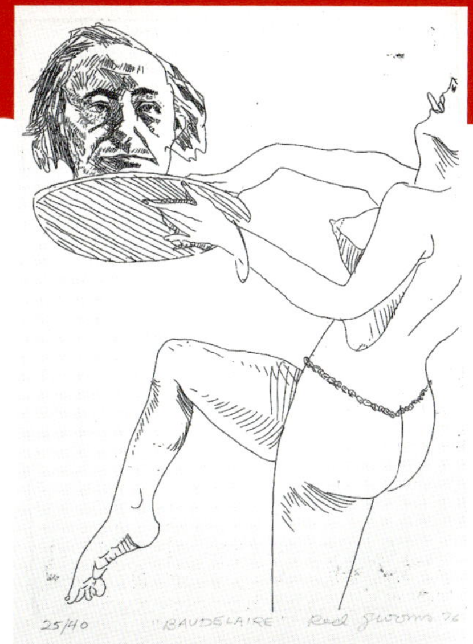

In his discussion,

Baudelaire conceded his debt to a short story titled "The Man of the Crowd" by Edgar Allan Poe, a writer whom the French poet had translated and who he considered to be "the most powerful pen of this day."[9] This acknowledgment of the famed American writer—a true spiritual ally for Baudelaire if there ever were one—provides a convenient and revealing segue back to our discussion of Grooms, who similarly cites the Poe piece as a formative influence on his work. In Poe's haunting tale, as Grooms himself recounts,

Could it be that Grooms is attracted to this story for the very same reasons that Baudelaire was—namely, that both find in the "man of the crowd" the perfect alter ego for the contemporary artist enamored by, indeed conversant with, the spectacle of the crowd? It is telling that the artist turned his thoughts to Baudelaire and to the portfolio of nineteenth-century artists at a rather quiet moment immediately following the uproarious hullabaloo—both in terms of physical exertion and critical response—that accompanied his best-known piece, *Ruckus Manhattan* (1975-76).[11] Created at the dawning of the artist's mid-life, the extravagant walk-through recreation of New York City's signature monuments had been in his mind, the artist attests, for ten years. The work in many ways embodies Baudelaire's definition of modernity: sited in the locus of the urban, engaged with the crowd, flamboyantly celebrating the present moment, and thoroughly immersed in the movement that lies at the heart of life in the modern metropolis. How is it that Grooms, a relatively small-town boy who moved to Manhattan as a young adult, became an artist of the city, that man of the crowd sung of by Poe and Baudelaire? How, in other words, did the ruckus—Grooms' synonym for the chaos of modern urban life—begin?

Charles Rogers Grooms

was born in 1937 in Nashville, Tennessee, a city then as now given to eclecticism and excess and unexpectedly home to one of the world's finest collections of Baudelairiana—a fact that the artist finds ridiculously wonderful.[12] As a boy, the budding artist staged backyard circuses and puppet shows inaugurating his love for the boisterous humor typically associated with such entertainment. "Growing up in Nashville in the 1950s," Grooms recalls, "I felt

Red Grooms

cooped up, locked into every kind of straitjacket you can imagine...I was pretty clear that I was going to be an artist, which is a fairly regular variety of oddball."[13] After high school, where classmates voted him "most witty," Grooms studied art at a variety of schools, including the School of the Art Institute of Chicago. By 1957 he was studying with Hans Hofmann, one of the luminaries of Abstract Expressionism, in Provincetown, Massachusetts. It was there, while working as a dishwasher at a local restaurant, that he was nicknamed "Red"—a moniker inspired by his carrot-top hair.

The apprenticeship with the legendary Hofmann, who found Grooms' work "too doll-like," was nonetheless crucial for the aspiring young artist. After a brief foray into abstraction, he came to the realization that something was lacking. "It wasn't really where my imagination lies. Maybe there was a storytelling and literary element in my mind that I couldn't give up."[14] Despite a taste for the painterly exuberance of Abstract Expressionism, Grooms turned away from the movement's lack of recognizable subject matter and pretensions to mythic grandeur, finding in its abstract depths a frustrating void separating art from the life around him.

Like many artists

of his generation—Andy Warhol and Claes Oldenburg among them—Grooms was ultimately committed to incorporating images of everyday life into his art, though he was never able to embrace the "cool," impersonal style associated with the Pop Art movement. Grooms, who had moved permanently to New York City by the late 1950s, turned his creative energies to this quest for the real and became a pioneer of "Happenings." During the next few years, in a series of absurdist performances, the increasingly antic artist created sets, costumes, and stage actions, effectively conjoining his life and art for the amusement of an audience. A lifelong love for filmmaking grew out of such performances, as did Grooms' comic and improvisational attitude toward his craft.

By 1963 Grooms created his first "stickout," a painted sculptural relief depicting famous denizens of the Parisian art world at the turn of the century. No subject was too mundane for these comic tableaux, however, as the artist turned to the events and people in his life for inspiration. By 1967 Grooms was at work on the first of his massive "sculpto-pictoramas," his term for the mixed-media walk-through environments depicting America's great cities and pastimes. *City of Chicago*, built for Chicago's Allan Frumkin Gallery, filled a space twelve feet high by twenty-five feet square and was composed of painted and sculpted recreations of the city's architecture and notorious citizens, including everything from the "el" train and the Wrigley Building to Al Capone, Oscar Mayer, and Mrs. O'Leary's cow.

Over the next fifteen years, Grooms created several such sculpto-pictoramas, a number of them on a truly staggering scale. *Ruckus Rodeo*, commissioned by the Fort Worth Art Museum (now the Modern Art Museum of Fort Worth) in 1976 for a space some 100 feet wide, was inspired by that city's Southwestern Exposition and Fat Stock Show. Reflecting the artist's ongoing desire to be comprehensive in his search for a true-to-life realism, that installation featured a sixteen-foot-high recreation of a Brahma bull, clowns in barrels, injured cowboys, and even a rodeo queen on horseback.

Ruckus Manhattan, probably the artist's best-known environment—and one that he considers a "blockbuster idea"—was also completed in the mid-1970s, initially for an immense public exhibition space in an office building in the heart of Manhattan's financial district. Grooms' homage to the Big Apple—his "rainbow pano-picto-rama of the sights, sounds, smells, and shapes of America's biggest melting pot"[15]—brought together manic, at times dizzying, near-replicas of such familiar landmarks as the Statue of Liberty (wearing platform shoes), the Brooklyn Bridge, the World Trade Center, and a tourist-ridden Rockefeller Center. Also included in the predominantly wood and vinyl installation were a subway

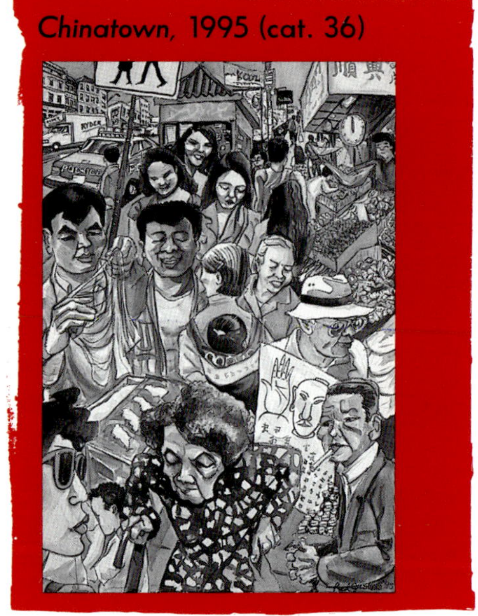

Chinatown, 1995 (cat. 36)

station and thirty-seven-foot-long subway car, complete with turnstile, over-life-sized passengers, and a spring-loaded floor. Some 50,000 New Yorkers traipsed through the ersatz urban environment, delighting in the familiar sights from their own concrete backyard.

Ruckus Manhattan was in many ways a defining moment in Grooms' career, though the artist's unabashed and ongoing love affair with the sights and sounds of New York—the "hometown of his sensibility"—has continued to the present day.[16] In the mid-1990s the artist almost single-mindedly devoted himself to *New York Stories*, a series of prints and sculptural tableaux dedicated to what he has called the "extraordinary texture" of the bustling metropolis. Featured in the visual stories are prominent architectural monuments, such as the Flatiron Building, and well-known Fifth Avenue landmarks including Saks, the Plaza Hotel, and St. Patrick's Cathedral. In his boisterous *Rockefeller Center*, a color lithograph from 1995, buildings open up and subterranean passages are exposed to the light of day revealing the milling masses that make up the human fabric of the city. Another equally teeming neighborhood appears in *Looking Up Broadway, Again* (1993), a color lithograph that captures in vivid detail the Canal Street environs in the vicinity of the artist's studio. Throughout *New York Stories*, one indeed senses Grooms the *flâneur* exploring the city in a magnificent stroll beginning at one end of Manhattan

Continued on page 17

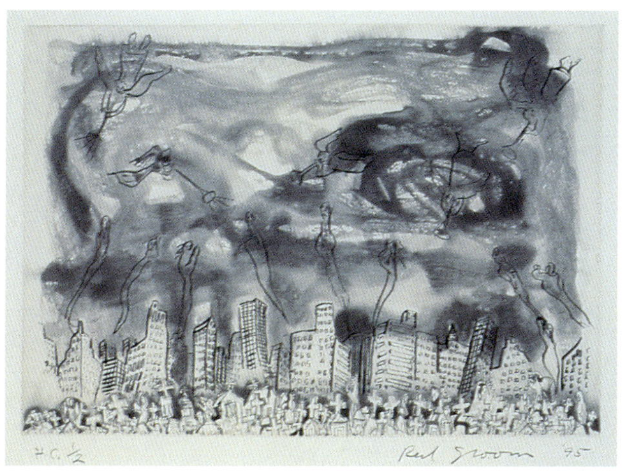 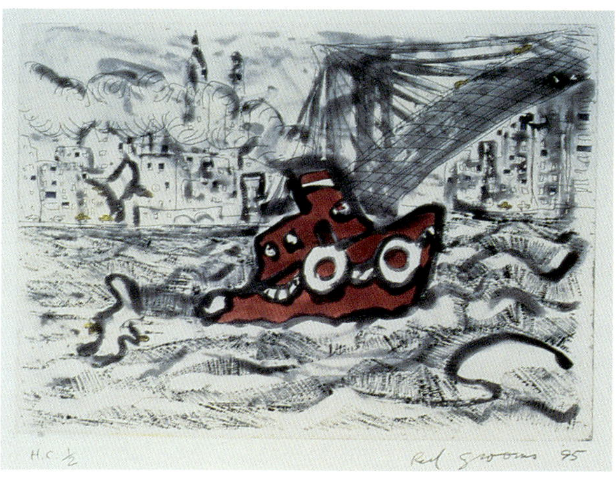

New York Sweet: Graveyard Ruckus, 1995
(cat. 28)

New York Sweet: Tootin' Tug, 1995
(cat. 31)

Saks Fifth Avenue, 1994 (cat. 12)

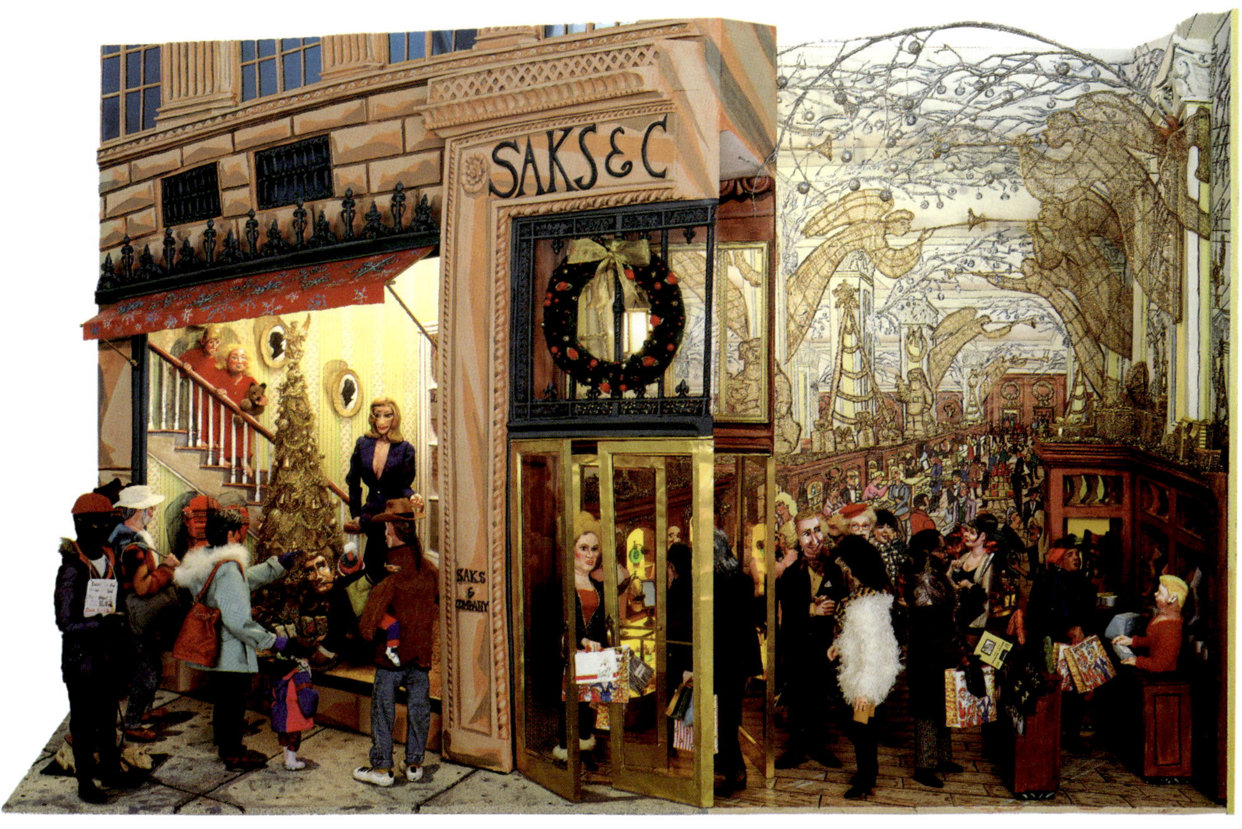

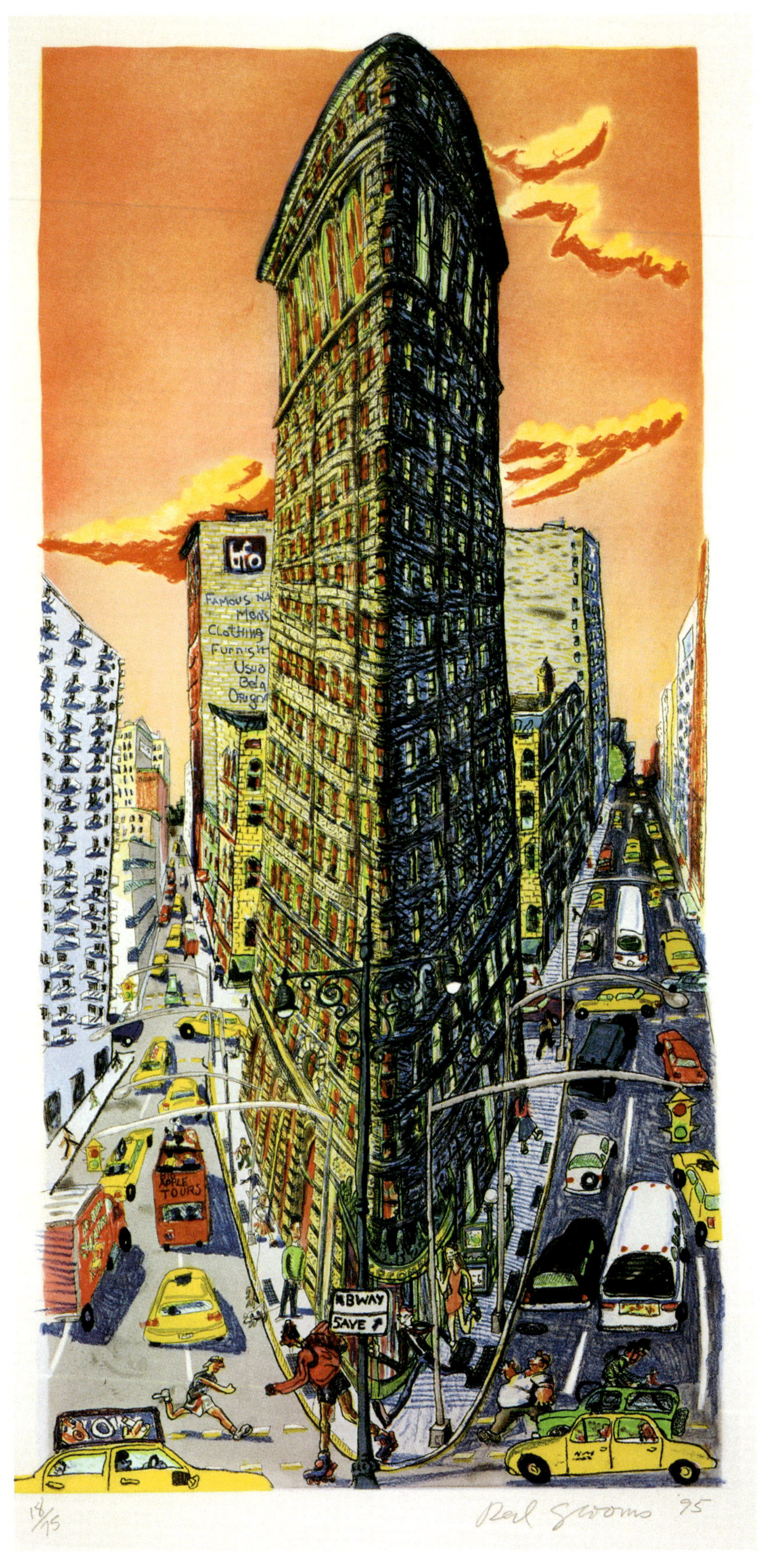

The Flatiron Building, 1995 (cat. 26)

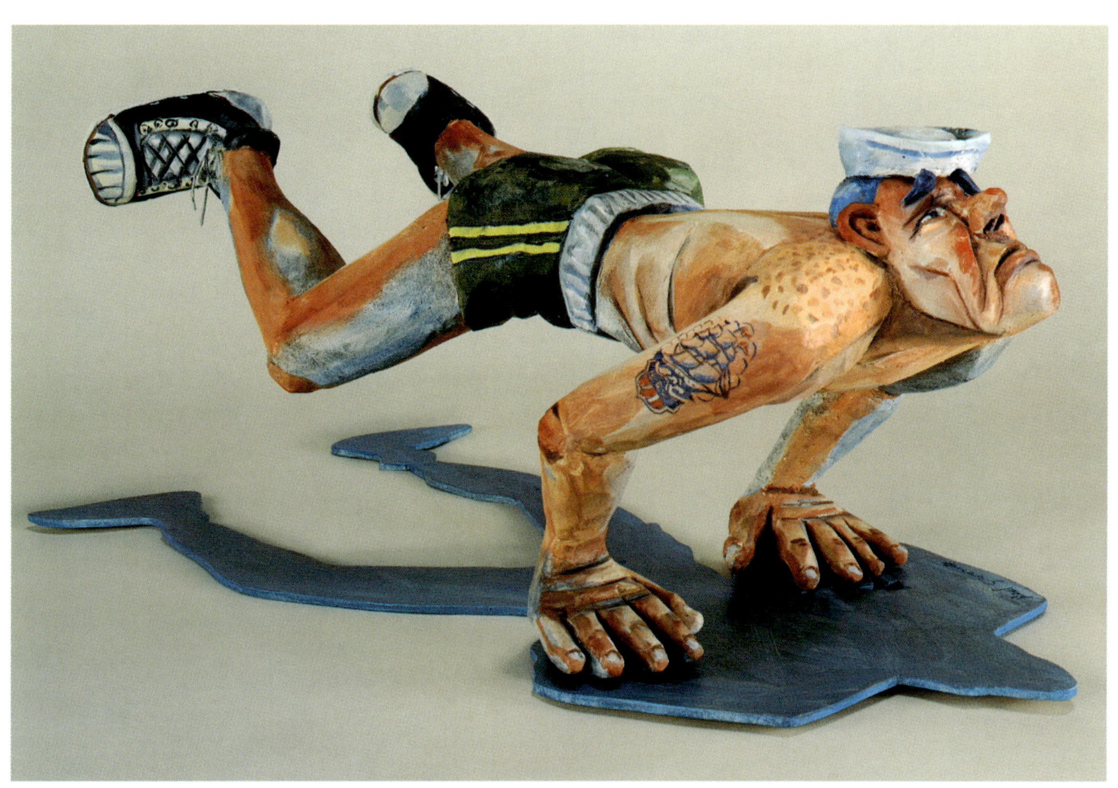

Muscle Beach Series: Sailor Kelly, 1989 (cat. 5)

Muscle Beach Series: Clean and Press, 1989 (cat. 2)

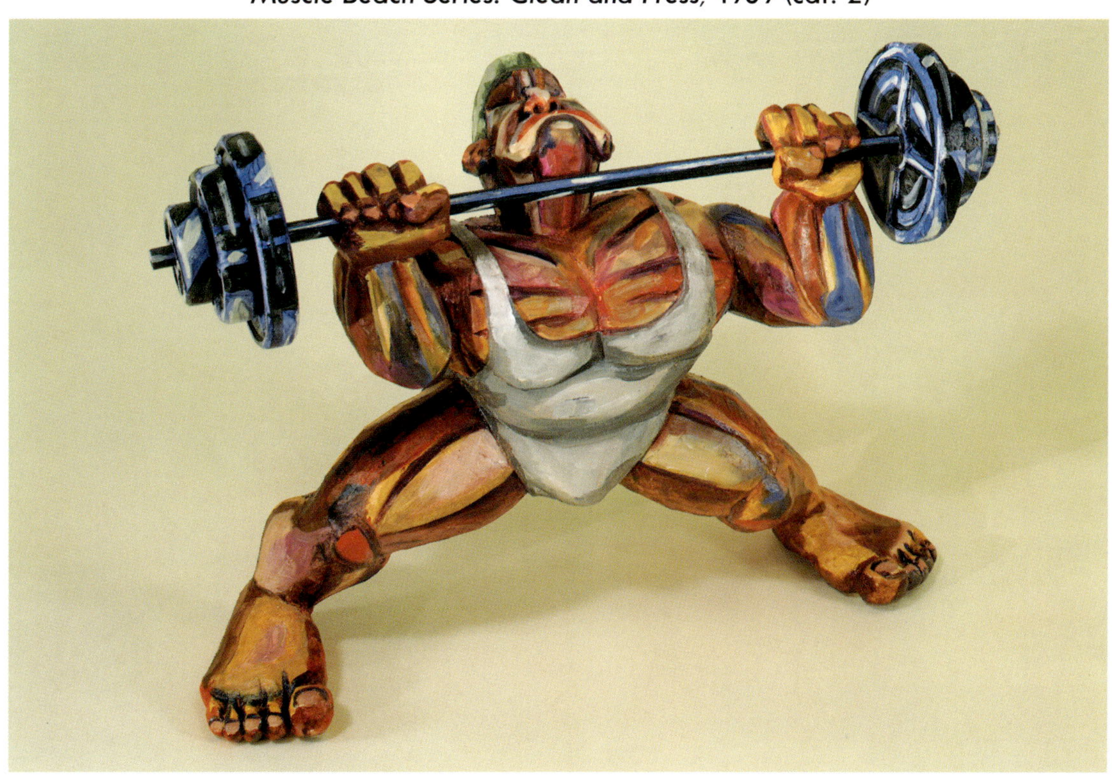

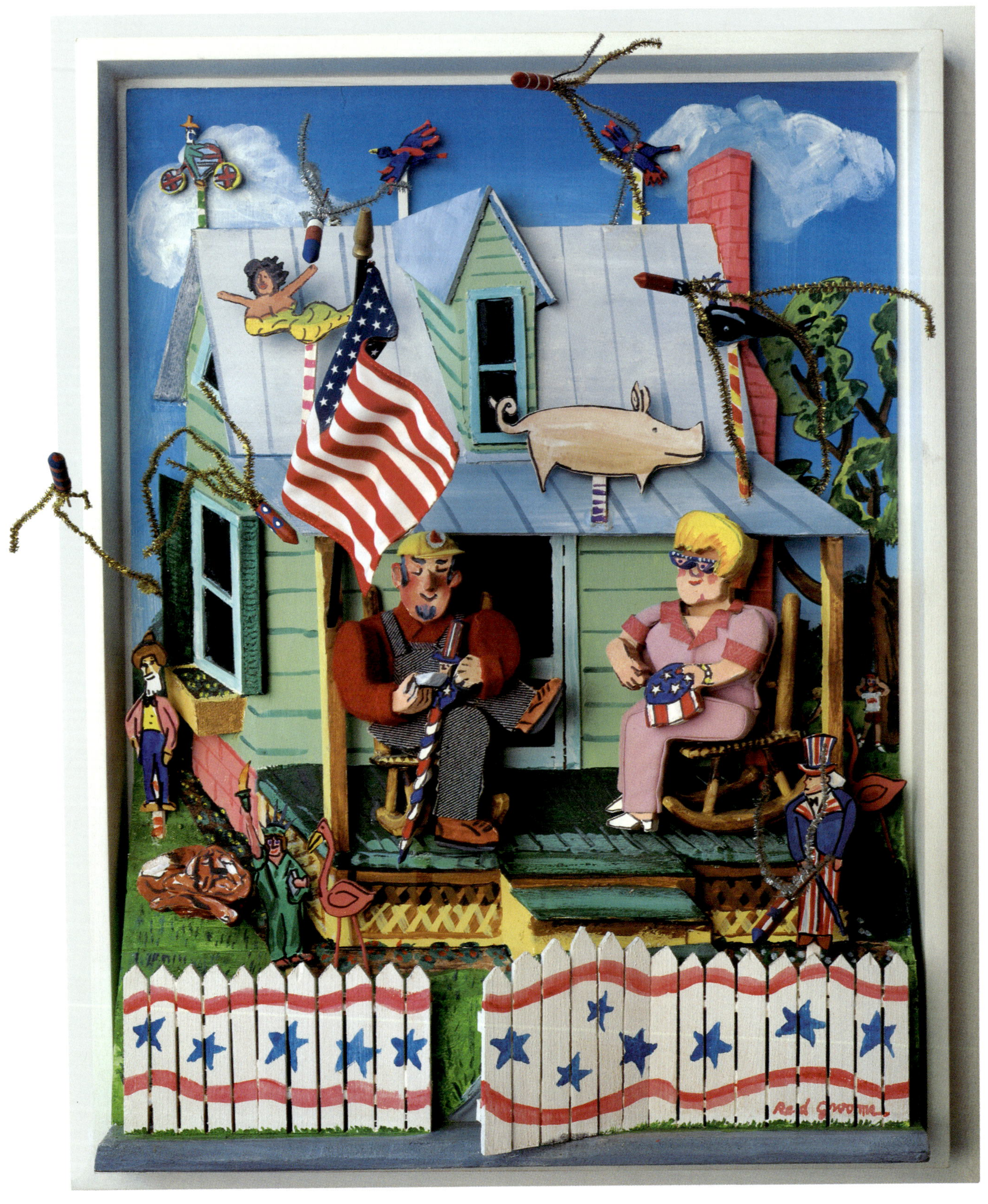

4th of July, 1993 (cat. 10)

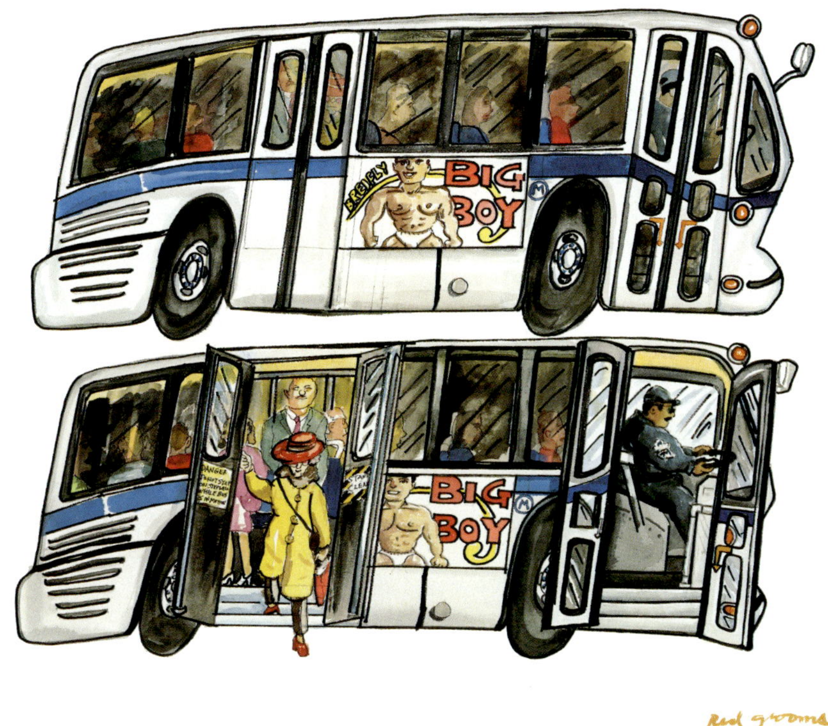

Study for The Bus, *1995 (cat. 38)*

Exact Fare, 1995 (cat. 37)

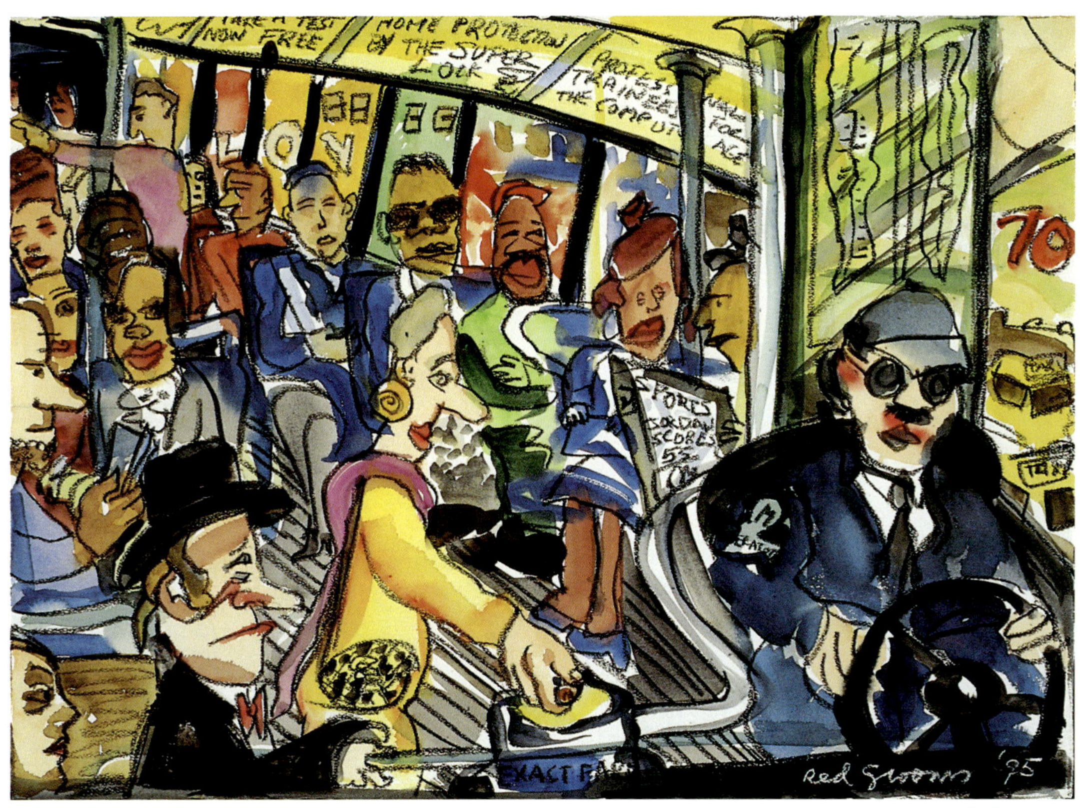

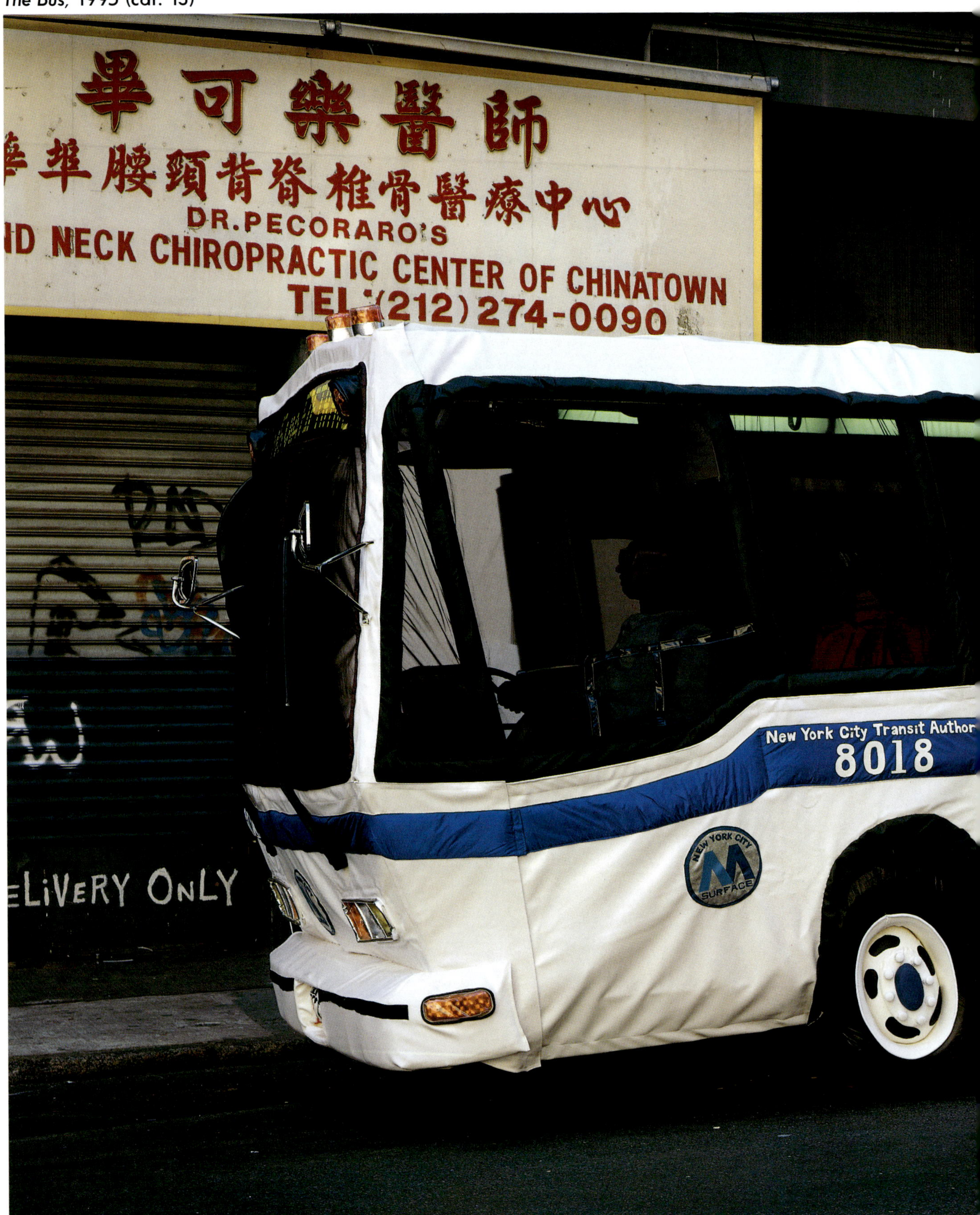
畢 可 樂 醫 師
華坪腰頸背脊椎骨醫療中心
DR. PECORARO'S
ND NECK CHIROPRACTIC CENTER OF CHINATOWN
TEL. (212) 274-0090
ELiVERY OnLY
New York City Transit Author
8018
NEW YORK CITY
M
SURFACE

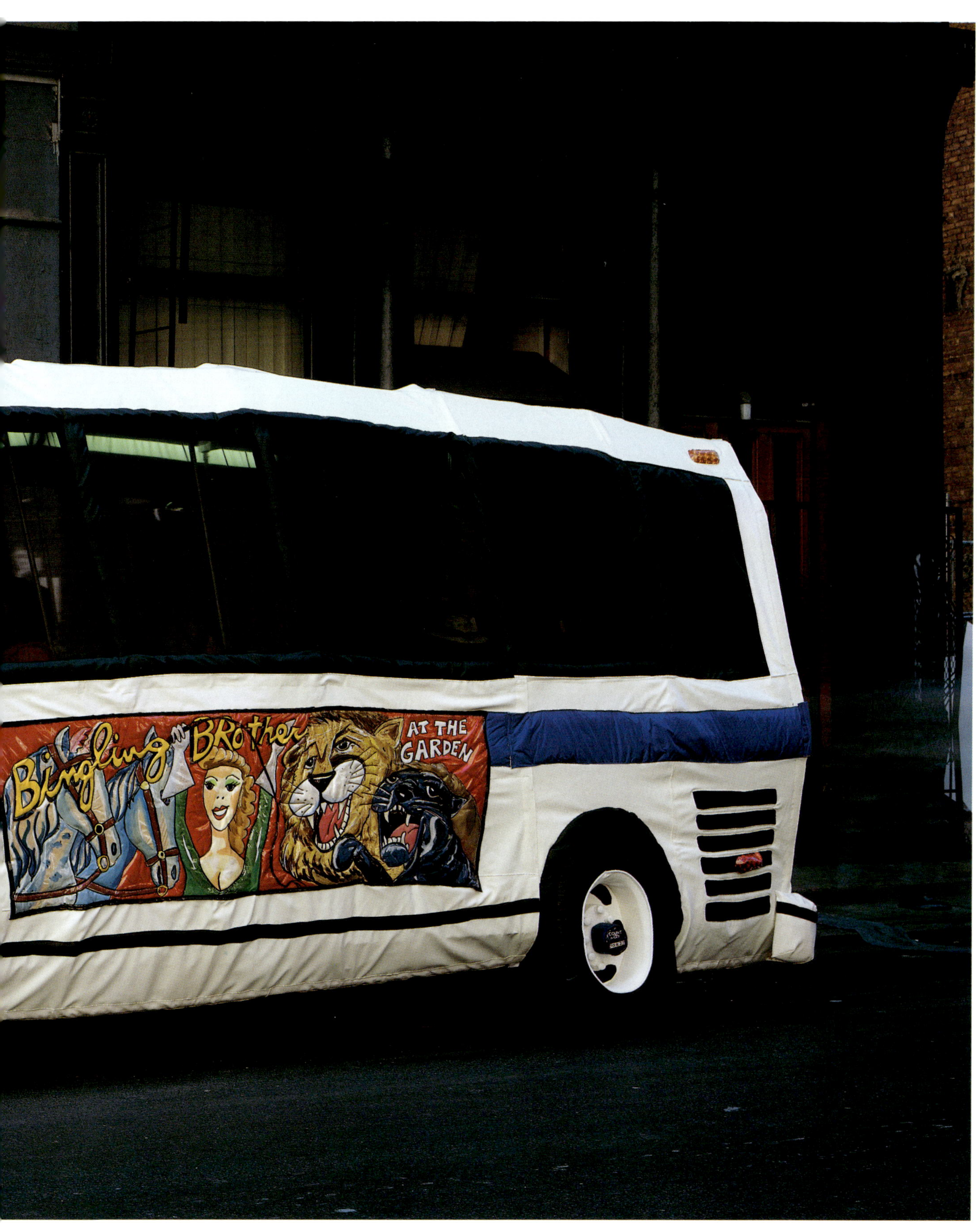

Ringling BRothers
AT THE
GARDEN

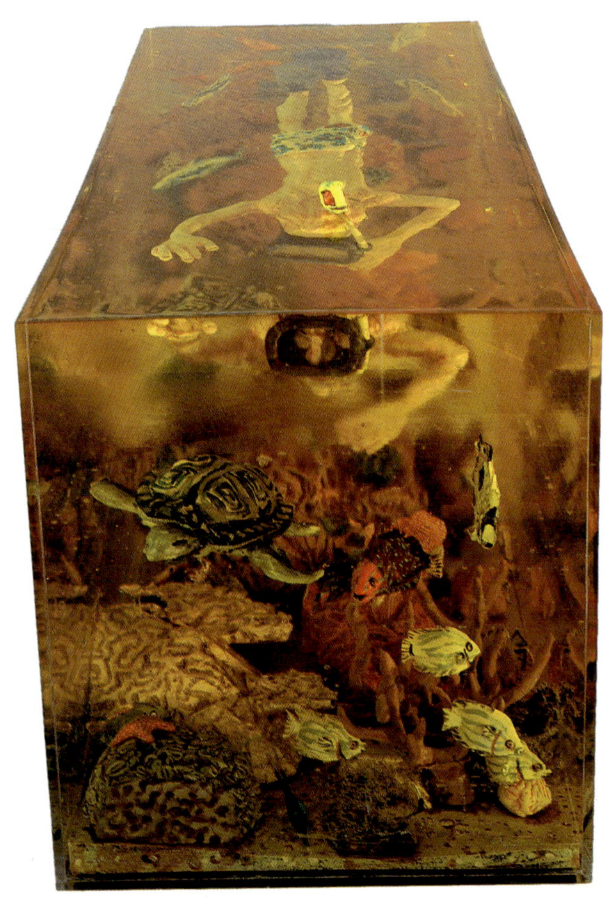

Snorklin' in Hawaii, 1990 (cat. 8)

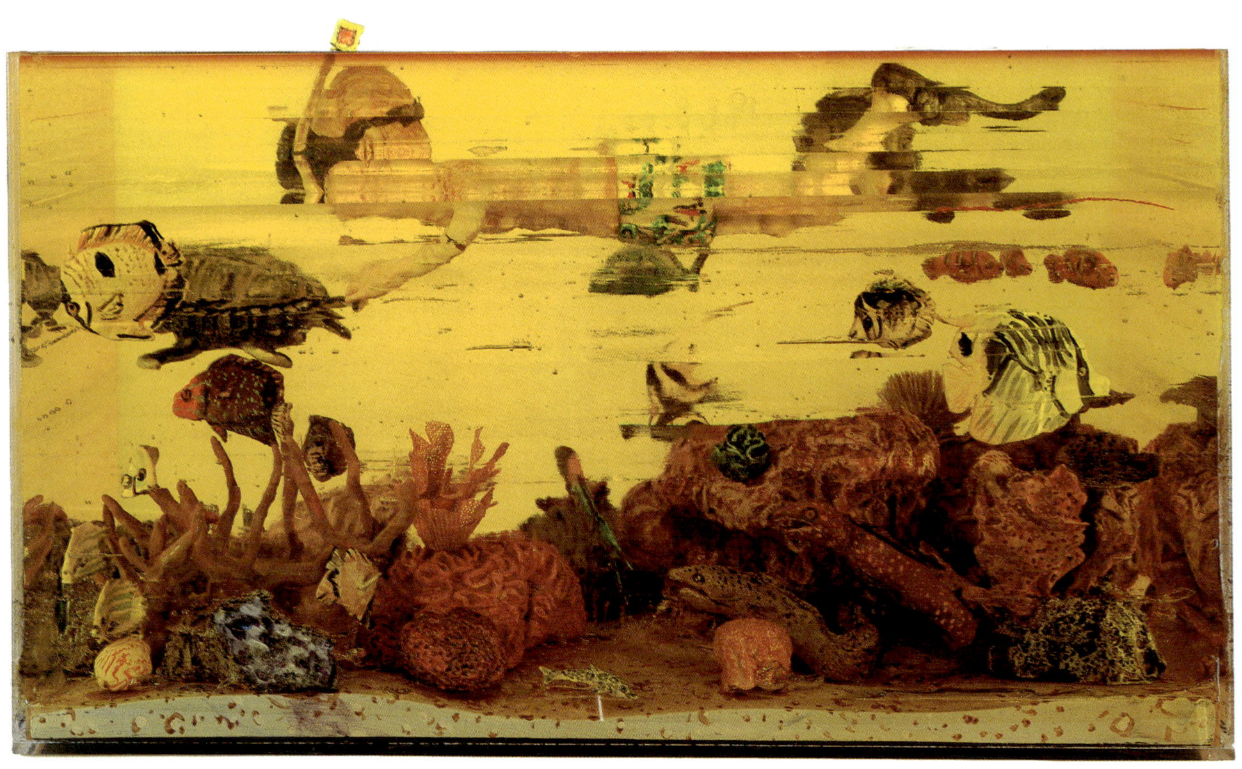

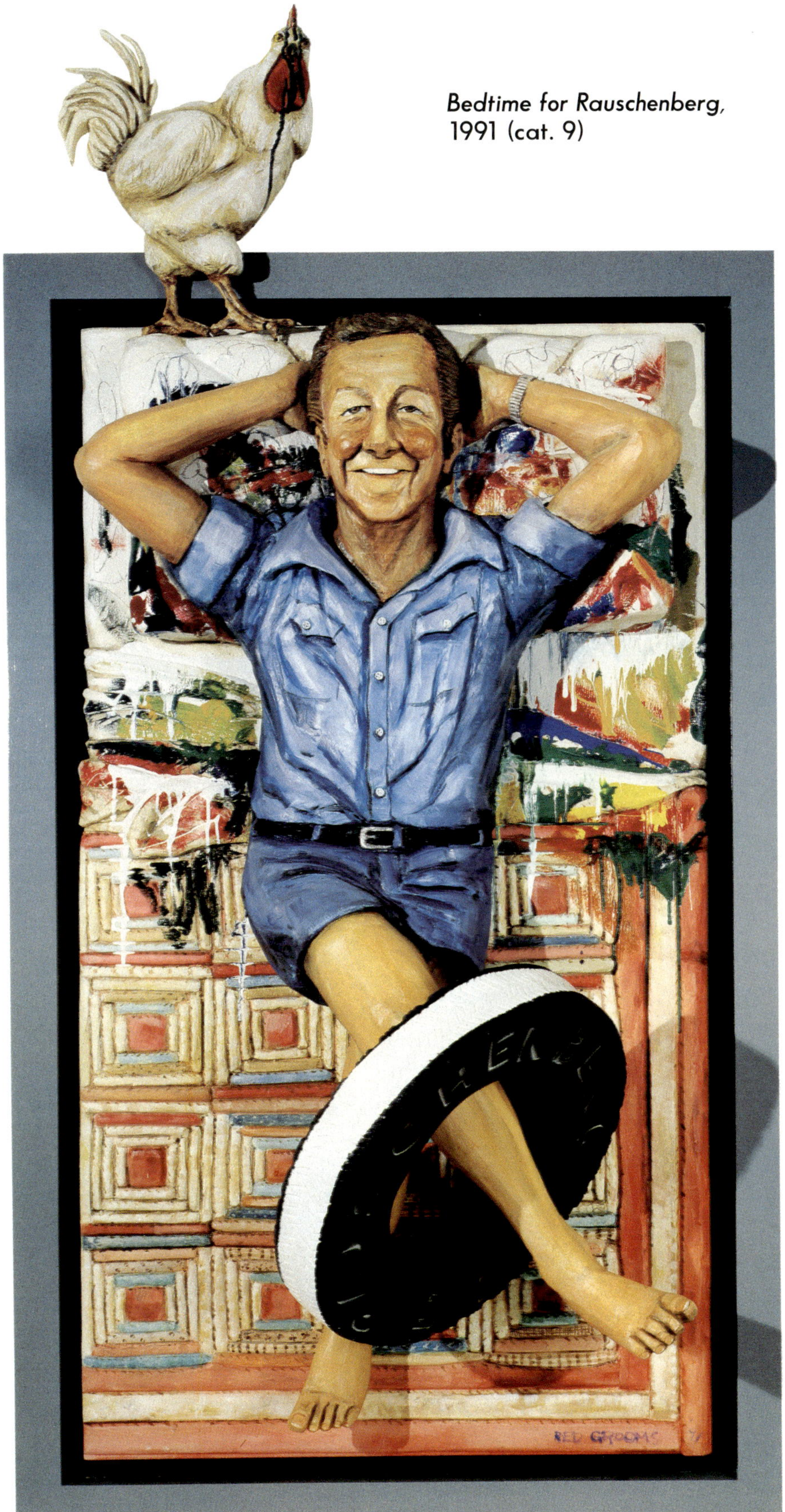

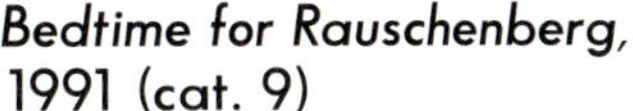

Bedtime for Rauschenberg,
1991 (cat. 9)

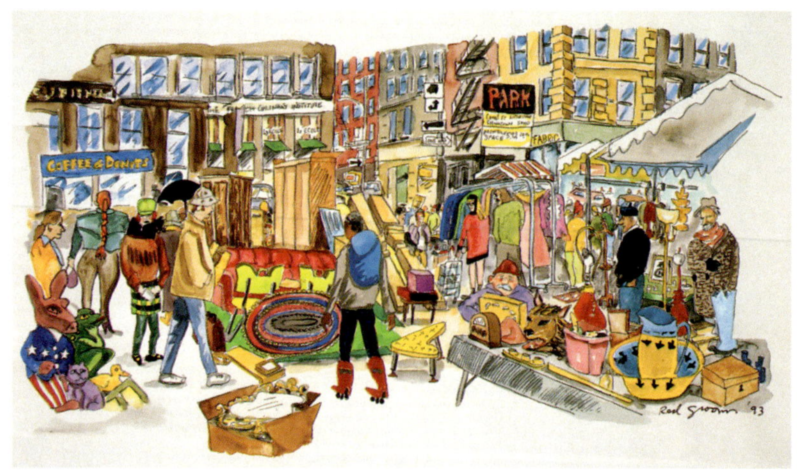

*Red Roller Blades,
Grand and Broadway
Flea Market, 1993
(cat. 35)*

De Kooning Breaks Through, 1987 (cat. 22)

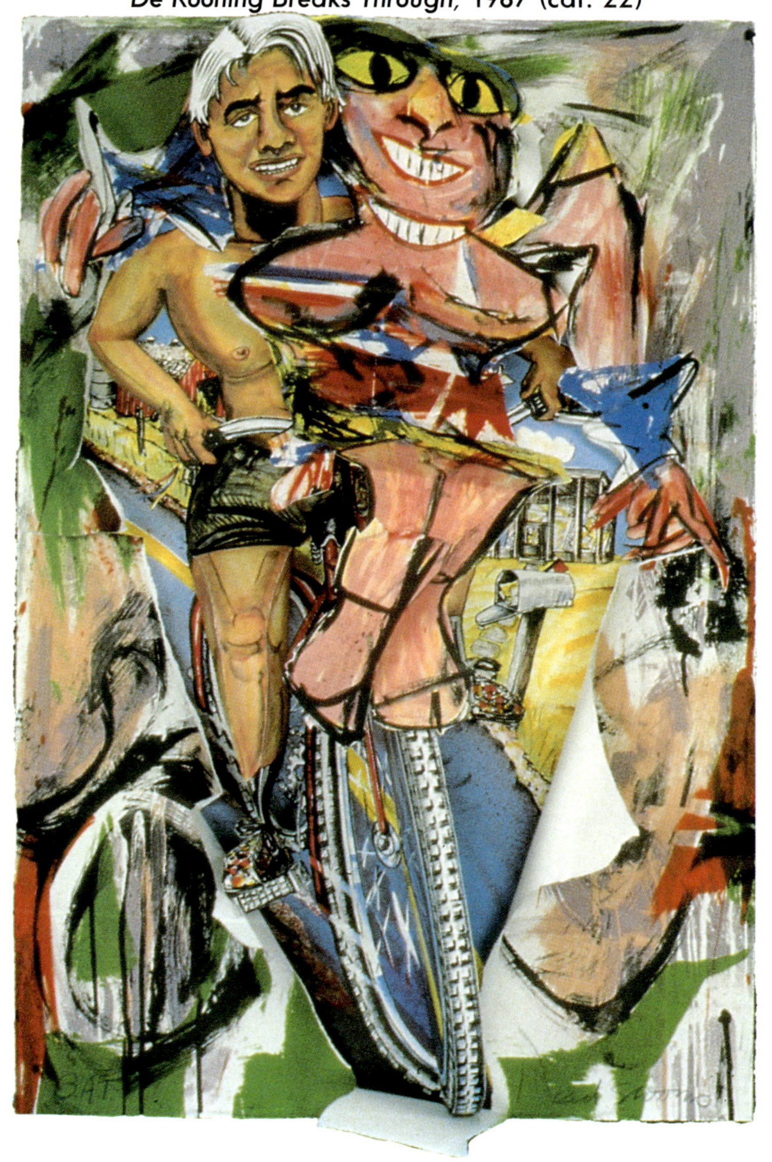

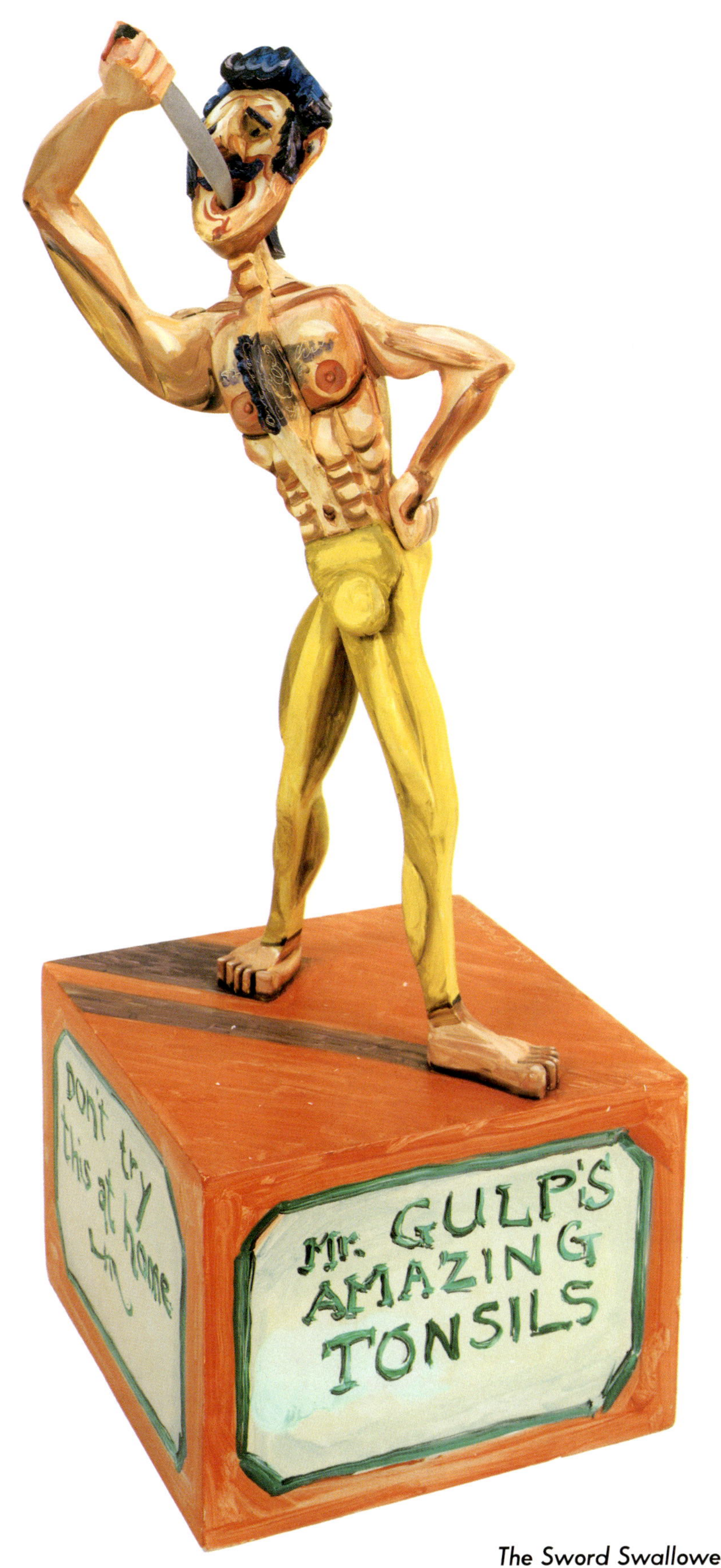

The Sword Swallower, 1997 (cat. 16)

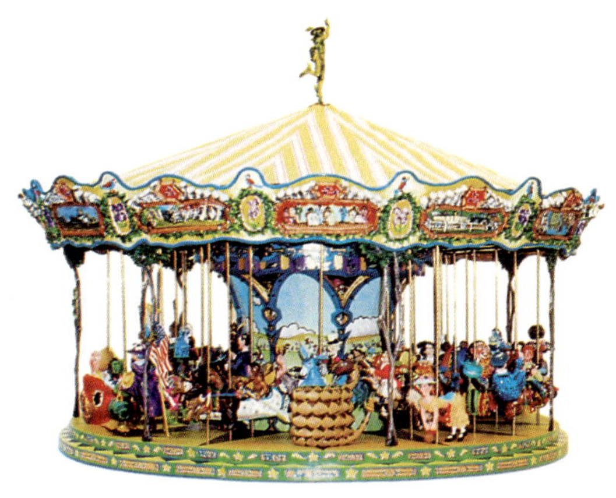

Model for Tennessee Fox Trot Carousel,
1994 (cat. 11)

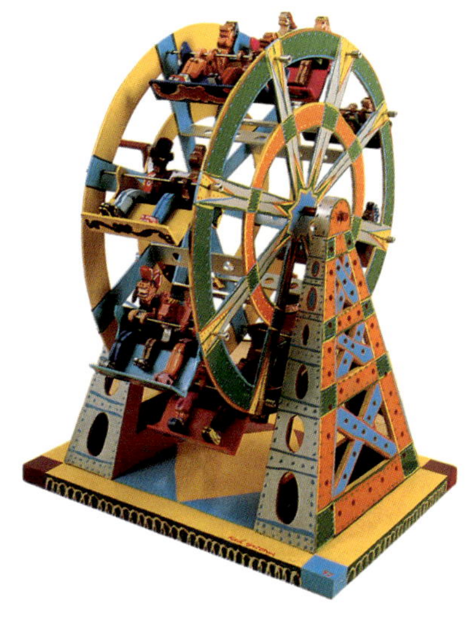

The Big Wheel, 1997
(cat. 15)

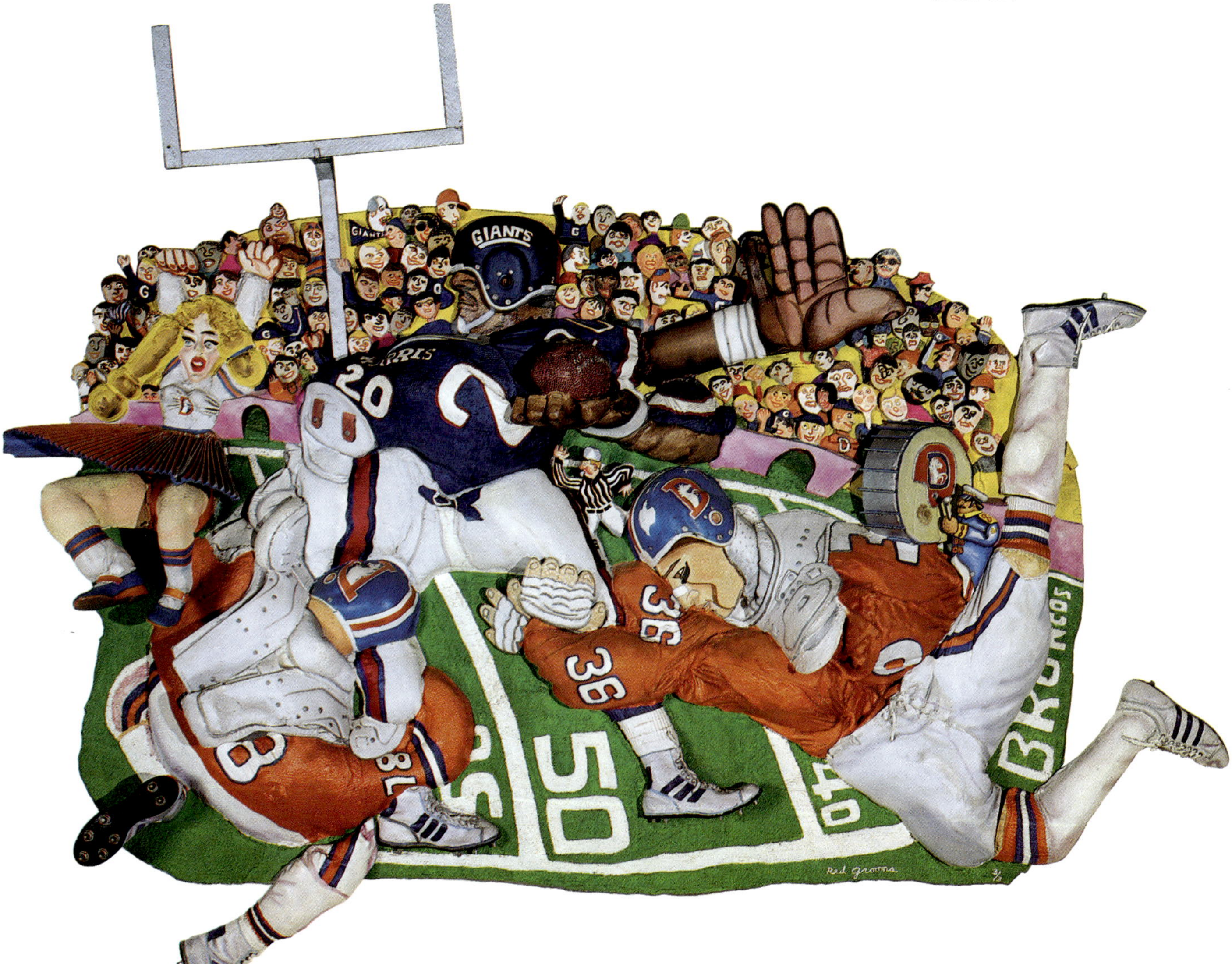

The Big Game, 1980 (cat. 1)

Continued from page 4

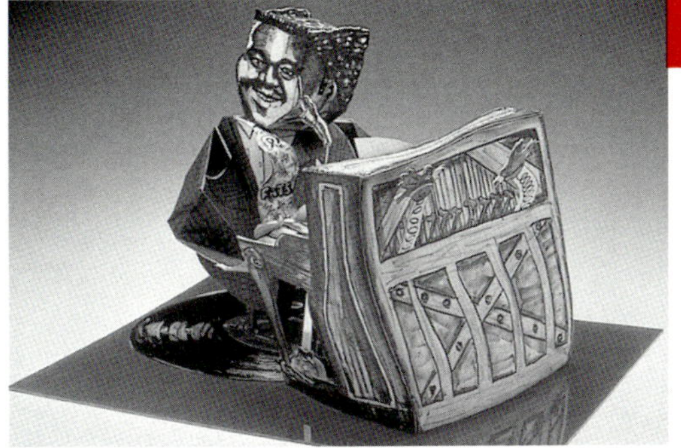

and ending at the other. His approach is that of the journalist on the prowl for street stories that will make good copy, and his attention to details of dress, physical type, signage, and locale is exhaustive and ultimately compelling. In pieces such as the Manhattan lithographs or *Saks Fifth Avenue* (1994), a mixed-media tableau, Grooms acknowledges

There's a terrific amount of information. It's like learning a part. If you know the part, you can take some liberties of expression with it. But I feel quite keenly that you should make the effort to know it. And you have to know it the way other people know it, so they can recognize their version in your version. Then I can fictionalize the work. I couldn't do it without the information.[17]

Surely Grooms—who uses drawing and throw-away cameras as *aide-mémoire*—would agree with Baudelaire that "every age has its own carriage, its expression, its gestures" that are crucial to the visual record of that particular era.[18] Indeed, the artist has concluded, "My goal is to make city people look as contemporary as I can, up to speed now, and throw some light on our time for the future."[19]

It has been said

that in its expansive scope Grooms' art is truly democratic. In *Saks Fifth Avenue*, for instance, salesgirls and street beggars almost literally rub noses with well-to-do patrons in a splendid homage to the commercial activity underpinning the urban spectacle. An altogether different venue—but one focused nonetheless on

Fats Domino, 1984 (cat. 19)

America's favorite pastime of shopping—can be found in *Red Roller Blades, Grand and Broadway Flea Market*, a pen and watercolor drawing from 1993. Shopping has here made its way into the streets, literally converging with the crowd so crucial to the city's familiar sense of chaotic energy. In *Chinatown*, a large gouache and litho crayon drawing from 1995, the procuring of goods commingles with the activity of eating in a crowded slice-of-life composition celebrating the ethnic flavors of the artist's own neighborhood.

That Manhattan is indeed a kind of smorgasbord (as opposed to a melting pot) of ethnic and social types is evident throughout Grooms' imagery of the city and is especially apparent in *The Bus* (1995), the extravagant piece at the spiritual center of *New York Stories*. The life-sized vinyl and nylon recreation of a city bus continues the artist's fascination with the often bizarre world of public transportation. Two decades earlier the subway and its world-weary passengers had been featured as an integral component of the *Ruckus Manhattan* ensemble of New York City monuments. In 1986 the underground transport system once again caught the artist's fancy in a hefty three-dimensional color lithograph titled *Subway*. With *The Bus* Grooms continues his exploration of the strange, anonymous intimacy fostered by communal travel. The denizens of this walk-through environment—including a bus driver whose head turns as a "passenger" enters—are (stereo)typical urban dwellers, their colorful garb a vivid reminder of the city's surfeit of visual information. The quotidian reality of a city bus—what Grooms calls "busness"—is remarkably rendered in the details of apparel, provocative advertisements, cautionary signage, and swaying floor. Baudelaire's understanding of modernity as a shifting or fluctuating simulacrum of the urban milieu is here gloriously embodied. *The Bus*, of course, is ultimately defined by movement as viewers enter, perambulate, and navigate the simulated terrain of modern urban existence.

Artists by a Railroad, 1996 (cat. 40)

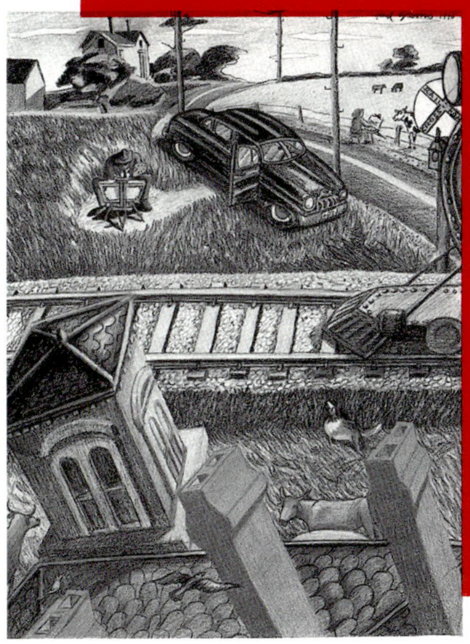

A more personal

side of Grooms' embrace of that urban terrain is amply evident in a recent series of five prints, *New York Sweet* (1995). The playful inversion of homonyms in the title clearly reveals the artist's longtime crush on his adopted hometown. The etchings grew out of an initial "practice session" with printmakers Carol Weaver and Felix Harlan, and the imagery in the series—ripe with personal associations for the artist—likewise evolved out of experimentation with the printmaking materials. The fluidity of *Graveyard Ruckus* suggests a rather open-ended generative process; in this instance, what grew out of the acid bath was one of Grooms' favorite views of Manhattan: the vista glimpsed from the Kosciuszko Bridge en route to the Brooklyn-Queens Expressway. "You've got this terrific view back toward Manhattan," the artist explains, "but you see it across the graveyard, which is always such a striking and awe-inspiring event . . . especially if you live in New York."

In *Hallelujah Hall* a similar fluidity gives way to a spirited, almost dancing St. John the Divine, the cathedral where Red and Lysiane Grooms were married in 1987. For Grooms the cathedral remains a personally significant Manhattan landmark because of its gift of shelter and humanity to the community. He also acknowledges that by not being European he "missed out . . . getting to do all those marvelous cathedrals."

The remaining works in the series, *Tootin' Tug*, *Down Under*, and *Piebald Blue* depict "iconic" images of the city for Grooms: tugboats, underground utility workers, and horse-drawn carriages at the Plaza Hotel.

Grooms' engagement

with modernity is, of course, not limited to the confines of the city but includes as well society's fascination with sports, fame, and entertainment. Scholars have suggested that the artist's oeuvre reveals an "ongoing search for heroes and heroines," from Hollywood stars and art world celebrities to sports figures and everyday workers.[20] The artist's visual homages to *Charlie Chaplin* (1986) and *Fats Domino* (1984), or to the anonymous sun worshippers of *Muscle Beach Totem* (1989), thus become an indelible part of what Baudelaire terms the "precious archives of civilized life."[21] Equal parts parody and praise, such works also interrogate our intense interest in the notion of celebrity. Through the years Grooms has remained fascinated by the everyday lives of famous artists in a series of works that effectively demystify their aura of sainthood. Legendary Abstract Expressionist Willem de Kooning thus rides a bicycle with one of his viraginous women, a motorized Frida Kahlo dances incessantly with Diego Rivera and Leon Trotsky, and straight-laced Piet Mondrian is forever locked in one of his own grids. *Bedtime for Rauschenberg* (mixed media, 1991) is a witty pastiche of a number of pieces by one of the great artists of the New York School, including his infamous *Bed* which utilized found objects—in this case, the artist's own pillow, quilt, and sheet. Rauschenberg, whose commingling of art and life is so similar to the philosophy of Grooms, reclines on his artistic detritus, joyfully at home with his "poetry of rubbish."[22] In a similar homey vein, *Artists by a Railroad*, a colored pencil drawing from 1996, provides a glimpse of Edward Hopper and his wife Jo peacefully painting in tandem at the site of one of the artist's most haunting works, *House by the Railroad* (1925). This image of domestic quietude is foreign to the ruckus of pieces such as *The Big Game* (aluminum, 1980); both nonetheless are records of how life was lived— documents, as it were, for the artist's "precious archives."

Red Grooms

In 1985 critic Judd Tully described Grooms' art as a kind of spinning "merry-go-round," an apt phrase that has turned out to be remarkably prescient.[23] Grooms has recently completed a full-sized operating carousel for Riverfront Park in downtown Nashville, the culmination of several years' work and his largest piece to date. This dynamic sculpto-pictorama— in which Davy Crockett and Andrew Jackson are transformed into fully ridable carousel figures—is a joyful tribute to the movers and shakers of Tennessee history and culture. For the artist, the *Tennessee Fox Trot Carousel* was a chance to pay homage to such local heroes and to return to his roots in the familiar territory of his natal city. The piece also represented a return to childhood and to the artist's youthful dreams of carnivals and circuses.

One's early work comes out of the genius of adolescence. It burns off as you become an adult. But you try and keep in touch with it all your life. It's important to become an adult, but you shouldn't lose the child either.[24]

Works such as the carousel and *The Big Wheel* (mixed media, 1997) are drawn from the artist's "childhood landscape."[25] Grooms vividly recalls his fascination with the people and accouterments of the state fair; as a teenager he even made a model of a carnival complete with banners announcing "Gulpo," a colorful character who reappears in a recent aluminum sculpture titled *The Sword Swallower* (1997).

The return to childhood at the heart of Grooms' art is yet another piece of evidence suggesting his place as a kind of modern commentator *à la Baudelaire*. For the poet, the true man of the crowd exhibits the sensibility of a convalescent or a child for whom the world is a constantly shifting spectacle of compelling sights and sounds.

Now imagine an artist perpetually in the spiritual condition of the convalescent, and you will have the key to the character of M.G. But convalescence is like a return to childhood. The convalescent, like the child, enjoys to the highest degree the faculty of taking a lively interest in things, even the most trivial in appearance . . . But genius is no more than childhood recaptured at will, childhood equipped now with man's physical means to express itself, and with the analytical mind that enables it to bring order into the sum of experience...[26]

Grooms is an artist

who possesses the genius of childhood, an artist, to quote Baudelaire once again, "for whom no edge of life is blunted." A perpetual spirit of wonder has throughout the years enabled him to take on the role of a contemporary *flâneur* who observes with enchantment the events, monuments, and people of his time. From this grand spectacle we call our modern world, Red Grooms distills the joyful, at times comic, essence, truly celebrating the heroism of modern life.

Joyce Henri Robinson
Associate Curator

Endnotes

1 Charles Baudelaire, "The Painter of Modern Life," in *Baudelaire: Selected Writings on Art and Artists*, trans. P.E. Charvet (Baltimore, 1972), 399-400. The essay was penned in 1859 and published in *Le Figaro* on November 26 and 29, and December 3, 1863.

2 Interview with David Shapiro in *Red Grooms: New York Stories* (Marlborough Gallery, 1995), 16.

3 Grace Glueck, "Odd Man Out: Red Grooms, the Ruckus Kid," *Artnews 72* (December 1973), 24.

4 As quoted in *Red Grooms*, exhibition catalogue (Knoxville Museum of Art, 1997), 15.

5 Charles Baudelaire, "The Salon of 1845," in *Art in Paris 1845-1862: Salons and Other Exhibitions Reviewed by Charles Baudelaire*, trans. Jonathan Mayne (Oxford, 1965), 32.

6 Charles Baudelaire, "The Salon of 1846," in *Baudelaire: Selected Writings*, 104.

7 "The Painter of Modern Life," 403.

8 "The Painter of Modern Life," 400.

9 "The Painter of Modern Life," 397.

10 Conversation with the author, July 17, 1998.

11 Throughout the portfolio, it has been noted, the artist "stifled the guffaws of his ruckus style." See Carter Ratcliff, *Red Grooms* (New York, 1984), 172.

12 The W.T. Bandy Center for Baudelaire and Modern French Studies, Vanderbilt University.

13 As quoted in *Red Grooms*, exhibition catalogue (Nagoya City Art Museum, 1993), 93.

14 As quoted in *Red Grooms* (Knoxville Museum of Art), 13.

15 Judd Tully, *Red Grooms and Ruckus Manhattan* (New York, 1977), 11.

16 Ratcliff, 32.

17 As quoted in *Red Grooms: New York Stories*, 12.

18 "The Painter of Modern Life," 404.

19 As quoted in *Red Grooms: New York Stories*, 24.

20 Ratcliff, 13; Barbara Haskell, *Ruckus Rodeo* (New York, 1988), n.p.

21 "The Painter of Modern Life," 435.

22 Daniel Wheeler, *Art Since Mid-Century: 1945 to the Present* (Englewood Cliffs, New Jersey, 1992), 128.

23 Judd Tully, "Red Grooms has artful fun with high culture—and low," *Smithsonian* (June 1985), 104.

24 As quoted in *Red Grooms: New York Stories*, 16.

25 The phrase is that of John Myers, one of Grooms' early dealers. Quoted in Glueck, 25.

26 "The Painter of Modern Life," 397-98.

Acknowledgments

The Palmer Museum of Art is delighted to present *Red Grooms and the Heroism of Modern Life*. We are indebted to Red Grooms and his wife, Lysiane Luong Grooms, for their enthusiasm for this project as well as their willingness to lend works to the exhibition. Janet M. Shein and Joseph D. Shein, Eugene Feldman, and Mr. and Mrs. William Schaffel also graciously lent objects from their private collections. The exhibition would not have been possible without the participation of Marlborough Gallery, New York. The Marlborough staff, especially Tara K. Reddi, Danielle Thornton, Kim Schmidt, Cynthia Garvey, Miki Watanabe, Stephen Bozler, and John Willis, were indispensable with preparations for the exhibition and catalog. Phillip Bruno, director, deserves special thanks for his crucial role in the initiation of the exhibition and for his continued support throughout the planning stages. Tom Burckhardt, Red Grooms' studio assistant, likewise served as an ongoing source of information and encouragement.

In addition to the photographs provided by Marlborough Gallery, John Lamka photographed the pieces in the artist's collection, and Paine/Pomeroy, Nashville, Tennessee, supplied images of the carousel. Photo/Graphics at Penn State photographed *The Flatiron Building* in the collection of the Palmer Museum.

Finally, to Jim and Barbara Palmer we extend our sincerest thanks for their generous support of the exhibition and catalog.

Jan Keene Muhlert
Director

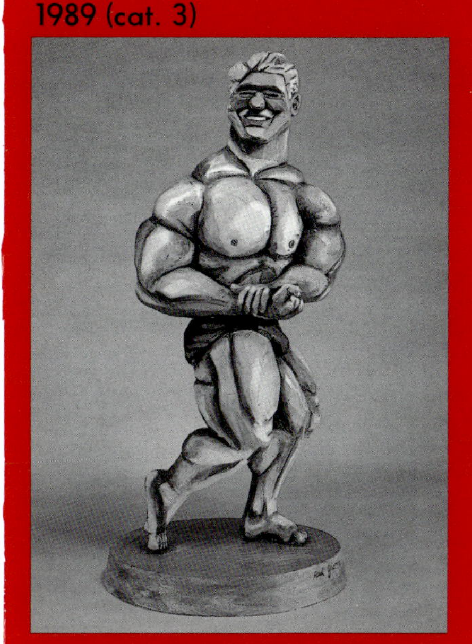

Muscle Beach Series: Mr. Universe,
1989 (cat. 3)

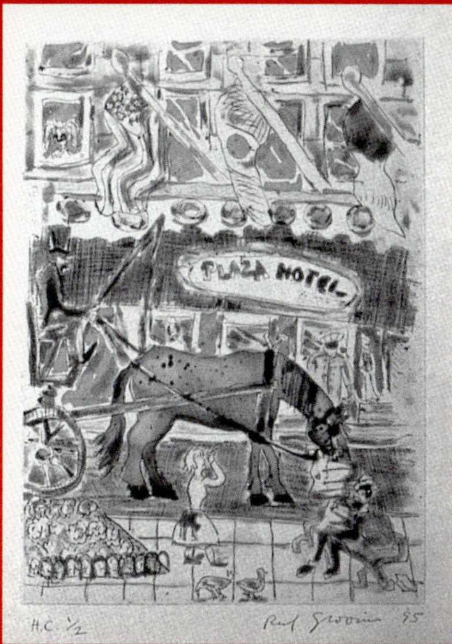

New York Sweet: Piebald Blue,
1995 (cat. 30)

Checklist of the Exhibition

MIXED MEDIA

1. *The Big Game*, 1980
   Painted aluminum
   96 x 101 x 17 inches
   Edition of 3
   Courtesy of Marlborough Gallery, New York

2. *Muscle Beach Series: Clean and Press*, 1989
   Painted bronze
   21 1/2 x 29 x 8 inches
   Edition of 9
   Courtesy of Marlborough Gallery, New York

3. *Muscle Beach Series: Mr. Universe*, 1989
   Painted bronze
   31 1/4 x 14 3/4 x 14 3/4 inches
   Edition of 9
   Courtesy of Marlborough Gallery, New York

4. *Muscle Beach Series:
   Muscle Beach Totem*, 1989
   Painted bronze
   41 x 15 x 10 inches
   Edition of 9
   Courtesy of Marlborough Gallery, New York

5. *Muscle Beach Series: Sailor Kelly*, 1989
   Painted bronze
   11 x 27 1/2 x 12 3/4 inches
   Edition of 9
   Courtesy of Marlborough Gallery, New York

6. *Frida's Cuckoo Clock*, 1990
   Enamel on wood, electric motor, tape recorders
   83 x 53 x 24 inches
   Courtesy of Marlborough Gallery, New York

7. *Mondrian*, 1990
   Painted bronze
   24 x 19 x 17 inches
   Edition of 9
   Collection of Red Grooms
   and Lysiane Luong Grooms

8. *Snorklin' in Hawaii*, 1990
   Ceramic and resin
   14 1/4 x 24 1/2 x 12 inches
   Collection of Red Grooms
   and Lysiane Luong Grooms

9. *Bedtime for Rauschenberg*, 1991
   Oil and enamel on wood
   95 x 49 x 27 inches
   Courtesy of Marlborough Gallery, New York

10. *4th of July*, 1993
    Wood and mixed media
    26 1/4 x 20 1/2 x 7 inches
    Collection of Red Grooms
    and Lysiane Luong Grooms

11. *Model for Tennessee Fox Trot Carousel*, 1994
    Mixed media, wood, lights, motor, sound
    30 x 42 inches diam.
    Collection of Red Grooms
    and Lysiane Luong Grooms

12. *Saks Fifth Avenue*, 1994
    Mixed media
    49 x 72 1/2 x 25 1/2 inches
    Courtesy of Marlborough Gallery, New York

13. *The Bus*, 1995
    Mixed media
    117 x 266 x 110 inches
    Courtesy of Marlborough Gallery, New York

14. *The Plaza*, 1995
    Mixed media
    70 x 92 x 18 inches
    Courtesy of Marlborough Gallery, New York

15. *The Big Wheel*, 1997
    Enamel on aluminum
    44 x 33 1/2 x 38 inches
    Edition of 2
    Courtesy of Marlborough Gallery, New York

16. *The Sword Swallower*, 1997
    Oil on aluminum
    42 x 16 x 15 inches
    Edition of 3
    Courtesy of Marlborough Gallery, New York

MULTIPLES

17. *Museum*, 1978
    Color lithograph
    10 1/4 x 23 3/4 inches
    Edition of 150
    Collection of Eugene Feldman

18. *Dali Salad*, 1980
    Color three-dimensional lithograph and
    silkscreen
    26 1/2 x 27 1/2 x 12 1/2 inches
    Edition of 55
    Collection of Janet M. Shein
    and Joseph D. Shein

19. *Fats Domino*, 1984
    Color three-dimensional lithograph
    17 x 17 x 20 inches
    Edition of 54
    Collection of Janet M. Shein
    and Joseph D. Shein

20. *Charlie Chaplin*, 1986
    Color three-dimensional lithograph
    23 x 18 x 11 inches
    Edition of 75
    Collection of Mr. and Mrs. William Schaffel

21. *Subway*, 1986
    Color three-dimensional lithograph
    14 1/2 x 40 3/8 x 7 inches
    Edition of 75
    Courtesy of Marlborough Gallery, New York

22. *De Kooning Breaks Through*, 1987
    Color three-dimensional lithograph
    42 3/4 x 28 5/8 x 6 3/4 inches
    Edition of 75
    Courtesy of Marlborough Gallery, New York

23. *Slam Dunk*, 1992
    Color three-dimensional lithograph
    21 3/8 x 18 1/8 x 12 1/2 inches
    Edition of 60
    Courtesy of Marlborough Gallery, New York

24. *Looking Up Broadway, Again*, 1993
    Color lithograph
    30 x 22 inches
    Edition of 75
    Courtesy of Marlborough Gallery, New York

25. *Taxi to the Terminal*, 1993
    Color lithograph
    22 x 30 inches
    Edition of 75
    Courtesy of Marlborough Gallery, New York

26. *The Flatiron Building*, 1995
    Color etching
    45 x 26 inches
    Edition of 75
    Purchased for the Museum by the Friends of the
    Palmer Museum of Art

27. *New York Sweet: Down Under*, 1995
    Color aquatint and sugarlift
    20 1/2 x 17 1/2 inches
    Edition of 30
    Courtesy of Marlborough Gallery, New York

28. *New York Sweet: Graveyard Ruckus*, 1995
    Drypoint, line etching, and aquatint
    17 1/2 x 20 1/2 inches
    Edition of 30
    Courtesy of Marlborough Gallery, New York

29. *New York Sweet: Hallelujah Hall*, 1995
    Line etching and aquatint
    17 1/2 x 20 1/2 inches
    Edition of 30
    Courtesy of Marlborough Gallery, New York

30. *New York Sweet: Piebald Blue*, 1995
    Color etching and aquatint
    20 1/2 x 17 1/2 inches
    Edition of 30
    Courtesy of Marlborough Gallery, New York

31. *New York Sweet: Tootin' Tug*, 1995
    Color line etching, etched roulette, and aquatint
    17 1/2 x 20 1/2 inches
    Edition of 30
    Courtesy of Marlborough Gallery, New York

32. *Rockefeller Center*, 1995
    Color lithograph
    41 3/8 x 27 1/2 inches
    Edition of 75
    Courtesy of Marlborough Gallery, New York

33. *Picasso*, 1996
    Color three-dimensional lithograph
    22 7/16 x 23 3/8 x 13 3/8 inches
    Edition of 75
    Courtesy of Marlborough Gallery, New York

OTHER WORKS ON PAPER

34. *Flea Market Grand and Broadway
    Man with Rug Beater*, 1993
    Pen and watercolor on paper
    19 3/8 x 17 inches
    Courtesy of Marlborough Gallery, New York

35. *Red Roller Blades, Grand and
    Broadway Flea Market*, 1993
    Pen and watercolor on paper
    13 1/2 x 22 inches
    Courtesy of Marlborough Gallery, New York

36. *Chinatown*, 1995
    Gouache and litho crayon on paper
    60 x 40 inches
    Courtesy of Marlborough Gallery, New York

37. *Exact Fare*, 1995
    Litho crayon and watercolor on paper
    22 1/4 x 30 1/8 inches
    Courtesy of Marlborough Gallery, New York

38. *Study for The Bus*, 1995
    Watercolor on paper
    22 1/4 x 30 1/8 inches
    Courtesy of Marlborough Gallery, New York

39. *New York Night Scene*, 1995-96
    Acrylic on paper
    24 1/2 x 40 inches
    Courtesy of Marlborough Gallery, New York

40. *Artists by a Railroad*, 1996
    Colored pencil on paper
    30 x 22 inches
    Courtesy of Marlborough Gallery, New York